D1046691

# Chinese Garden Pleasures

# Chinese Garden Pleasures
## An Appreciation

Alison Hardie

Better Link Press

This book is edited and designed by the Editorial Committee of *Cultural China* series

Compiler and Translator: Alison Hardie
Images and photographs: Shanghai Museum, Liaoning Provincial Museum, Quanjing, Getty, Imagine China
Designer: Wang Wei
Editor: Yang Xiaohe
Editorial Director: Zhang Yicong

Senior Consultants: Sun Yong, Wu Ying, Yang Xinci
Managing Director and Publisher: Wang Youbu

ISBN: 978-1-60220-145-3

Address any comments about *Chinese Garden Pleasures: An Appreciation* to:

Better Link Press
99 Park Ave
New York, NY 10016
USA

or

Shanghai Press and Publishing Development Company
F 7 Donghu Road, Shanghai, China (200031)
Email: comments_betterlinkpress@hotmail.com

Printed in China by Shenzhen Donnelley Printing Co., Ltd.

1 3 5 7 9 10 8 6 4 2

*On page 2*

Peach blossom frames a view across Kunming Lake to the pagoda on the slopes of Longevity Hill in the grounds of Beijing's Summer Palace.

# Contents

*Introduction* 6

Environment 12

Visits and Connoisseurship 24

Feasting and Drinking 38

Water and Tea Tasting 46

Literati Pursuits 54

Drama 74

Boating and Fishing 82

Festivals 90

Plants and Animals 102

The Four Seasons 118

*Dates of the Chinese Dynasties* 128

# Introduction

The gardens of late imperial China (the Ming and Qing dynasties, mid-14th to 19th centuries) were sites where the elite culture of China's scholar-officials was displayed in its fullest glory, but gardens might also be owned by wealthy merchants or even by high-class courtesans, and even the gardens of the upper class were sometimes open to the public, particularly at festival times, so an enjoyment of garden culture was shared across a wide social range. Gardens were used not just for the garden owner and his immediate family to relax in and feel close to the natural world, but for all sorts of activities, individual and social. These might include lantern displays, chess matches, poetry contests, drama performances, or the display and enjoyment of someone's collection of antique objects or paintings and calligraphy. They were both an extension of the dwelling house, including many small buildings which could be used for relaxing, writing, eating or sleeping, and a contrast to the dwelling house. The house was quite rigidly and regularly arranged, with its inhabitants assigned living quarters according to their rank and status within the extended family, while the relatively irregular layout of the garden provided a space in which status hierarchies could be

◀ Two young men enjoy a game of cards in a garden environment among the spring greenery of a public park.

temporarily forgotten or at least set aside. It was a space which owed more to the "free and easy" ideals of Taoism than to the ritual and protocol of Confucianism. Ideally, it was a complete microcosm, "manifesting the large within the small," as well as a representation of the magical realm of the immortals, in which the garden owner could imagine himself also as an immortal freed from the trammels of everyday life and routine. Gardens would be designed to recall these magic realms, for example by representing the three islands of the immortals in the Eastern Sea in the form of three rocks or islets within a pond, and by giving the illusion of infinite extent by a cunning arrangement of separate but linked spaces which would draw the visitor on without ever revealing a complete view of the whole. "Borrowed views" of architectural or landscape features beyond the boundaries of the garden would add to this illusion of limitless extent.

The growth of the Chinese economy in the 16th century led to a culture of leisure and conspicuous consumption which encouraged the development of gardens both as a form of conspicuous consumption in themselves—moralistic authors wrote disapprovingly about the amounts of money and labor expended on bringing in massive rocks to build impressive

▶ Gardens have always been settings for the performing arts as well as for solitary contemplation of nature. In this garden a stage awaits musicians or a story-teller, with tables and chairs set up before it for the audience who will enjoy drinking tea and chatting as well as listening to the performance.

▲ *Beauties* (Chuiwan)
Du Jin (15th – 16th century), Ming dynasty
Handscroll, colour on silk
Height 30.5 cm, width 168.9 cm

This work recreates that of an "old master," Zhou Wenju (active 961 – 975), whose *Court Life* depicted various aspects of the daily life and entertainment of the imperial concubines. Here the ladies are shown playing *chuiwan* in the garden. *Chuiwan* was a ball game popular from the Song and Yuan periods where the players tried to hit a ball into a hole, similar to western golf. It was very popular among Ming aristocrats. The painting shows a ball which has stopped right next to the hole. The player lowers her head and bends her knee, with her club hand extending out: she has just missed her putt!

rockeries or "artificial mountains"—and as sites for the display of other forms of conspicuous consumption such as antique collecting or performances by privately-owned drama troupes. For many centuries landscape painting had been regarded as one of the highest forms of art, as well as a substitute for distant travel: later writers often quoted the painter Zong Bing (375 – 443) who painted landscapes on the walls of his room when he was too old to travel, so that he could enjoy what he called "recumbent wandering." Gardens could be conceived as three-dimensional landscape "paintings" in which the owner and his guests could enjoy this relaxing form of "sight-seeing." Designers of gardens could draw not only on China's rich visual arts tradition but also on the literary tradition to enrich the meaning of the garden through the use of allusion or by positioning calligraphic inscriptions which would guide the viewer's response.

In a rapidly urbanising society, gardens provided a way to escape from the social, material and psychological pressures of city life into an idealised rural environment. No wonder that the better-off, whether they were garden owners themselves or urban residents with access to other people's gardens, chose to entertain themselves with festive lantern displays, with music, poetry, art, theatre and other cultural activities. The pages which follow contain a flavor of these delights in the form of poetry and prose by writers of the Ming and Qing, together with some of the classic early texts which influenced them, illustrated by paintings, prints and objects which reflect the richness of Chinese garden culture.

# Environment

Chinese writers were always ready to express their opinions about the ideal garden environment, whether it was an enclosed dwelling in the middle of a bustling city or a secluded retreat out in the countryside—but not too far from congenial friends and the cultural life of the city. Sometimes they liked to laugh at their own inability to stop adding more and more refinements to their ideal environment; at other times they were enjoyed observing the progression of the four seasons bringing spring green or autumn red to the vegetation around them. Sometimes, too, the sight of a garden fallen into disrepair would stir memories of happier days.

◀ During imperial times, Hangzhou's West Lake functioned as a public park for the inhabitants of the city, and was thronged with visitors on festival days. It was also the location of many private gardens belonging to prominent local families. The area around the lake became known for ten famous scenic views, which were canonised by the Qianlong Emperor in the 18th century. Here we see the site known as "Watching the fish in the Flower Harbour."

Thus pavilions and terraces have feelings of the untrammelled scholar, chapels and belvederes the charms of the recluse. One must plant fine trees and rare bamboos, display epigraphic specimens, books and pictures. Thus the dweller will forget his aging, the sojourner there will forget to go home, the wanderer there will forget his weariness. In hot weather there will be cooling zephyrs; in freezing times there will be cheering warmth. If one indulges in extravagant earthmoving and planting, valuing colourful effects, then it becomes like a fetter, a mere cage.

—Wen Zhenheng, *A Treatise on Superfluous Things*; translation by Craig Clunas, *Fruitful Sites*, Reaktion Books, 1996, pp.93-94

Wen Zhenheng (1585 – 1645), was a writer and painter from one of the great families of Changzhou (present day Suzhou) in the late Ming dynasty. His *A Treatise on Superfluous Things* is a manual of taste expressing his aesthetic views on a wide variety of aspects of elegant living.

▲ *Mountain Scene with Human Figures*
Qing dynasty
Jade
Length 29.2 cm, width 6.5 cm, height 19 cm
Shanghai Museum

▲ *Reading at the Window in Autumn*
Liu Songnian (1127 – 1279)
Southern Song dynasty
Ink and colour on silk
Height 25.8 cm, width 26 cm
Liaoning Provincial Museum

…I spent most of my time in the study reading my books. ... When mind and body were both weary, I could cast my rod and catch fish, or gather herbs in my skirt, or open the channels to irrigate my plants, or wield an axe to chop down bamboo, then bathe my hands in warm water, and climb to a high place and gaze as far as my eyes could see, wandering freely exactly as I wished. The bright moon would appear at the appointed time, the fresh breeze would arrive of its own volition. There was nothing to drag me along and nothing to impede me; my ears, eyes, lungs and guts were all under my own control, alone and uninhibited. I don't know what other pleasure there is between heaven and earth that can take the place of this. So I named the whole place "The Garden of Solitary Delight."

—Sima Guang, *Record of the Garden of Solitary Delight*

Sima Guang (1019 – 1086), a historian, scholar and high chancellor of the Song dynasty.

In the winding rooms and secret buildings where Li Xiangzhen, known as Tenth Lady Li, lived, there were screen-curtains and the finest antique vessels everywhere. Within, she had built a long gallery; to the left of the gallery was planted a single old prunus tree. When it was in flower, fragrant snow [prunus blossom] drifted over table and couch. To the right of the gallery were planted two paulownia trees and ten or so stems of giant bamboo. Morning and evening she washed the paulownias [in emulation of the painter Ni Zan] and wiped the bamboos; their viridian colour was positively edible. People who visited her house wondered whether they had left the world of dust.

—Yu Huai, *Miscellaneous Reminiscences of Plank Bridge*

Yu Huai (1616 – 1696), writing in the early Qing, recalls the glamorous courtesans of the late Ming who inhabited Nanjing's pleasure quarters in the Plank Bridge neighbourhood.

▲ This painting is one of the many scenes depicted on the "Long Gallery" of the Summer Palace, one of the great imperial gardens of Beijing. It shows the great Yuan dynasty painter Ni Zan (1301 – 1374), who loved to paint paulownia trees, which he had planted around his studio. Obsessed with cleanliness, he made his page-boys wash the trees every morning under his supervision.

拙政园

When I first started construction, I meant to have a building of no more than three to five bays. Visitors kept pointing out that I could put a pavilion here or a gazebo there, to which I listened with indifference, under the impression that I had no such intention. But then, after I had wandered around a few times, unconsciously I began to lean towards my visitors' views, and became quite excited about them. It did indeed seem as though I could not do without this pavilion or that gazebo. Before one project was completed, my mind would unconsciously turn to yet another which I felt obliged to embark upon. Whenever a road or pathway came to an abrupt end, I racked my brains over it, and fashioned it anew in my dreams; then new areas would be opened up as if by the work of heaven.

—Qi Biaojia, *Notes on Allegory Mountain*

Qi Biaojia (1603 – 1645), a Ming statesman, bibliophile and drama theorist, was the owner and designer of Allegory Mountain (Yushan) or Allegory Garden (Yuyuan) in Shaoxing; here he describes the pleasures of planning his garden.

◀ A bird's-eye view of the Artless Administrator's Garden (*Zhuozheng Yuan*)

The old garden is a deserted, cheerless place;
Visiting it again, my longings are redoubled.
Throughout the garden the prunus is bursting into
white blossom;
On either bank the willows unfold their green.
The fragrant plants are burgeoning forth in clumps;
Rushing springs are audible wherever you are.
The evening crows hurry the sun towards dusk;
Returning, I go accompanied by the moonlight.

—Shang Jinglan, *Allegory Garden*

The poet Shang Jinglan, the wife of Qi Biaojia, visits the garden her husband created, long after the death of Qi. Nightfall reminds her not only of her much-loved husband's suicide in 1645, but of the collapse of the Ming dynasty which occasioned it.

▶ *Bamboo and Beauty*
Qiu Ying (? – c.1552)
Ming dynasty
Hanging scroll, ink and colour on silk
Height 166.8 cm, width 97.2 cm
Shanghai Museum

▲ *Zhenshang Studio*
Wen Zhengming
Ming dynasty
Handscroll, ink and colour on paper
Height 36 cm, width 107.8 cm
Shanghai Museum

The great Ming artist Wen Zhengming painted this in 1549, at the age of 80, for his friend the art collector Hua Xia; it is an idealised image of Hua's studio, the Studio of True Appreciation, and its surrounding garden.

# Visits and Connoisseurship

One of the pleasures of garden culture was to visit the gardens of others, either by invitation or simply by turning up and asking for admittance. Members of the educated class who prided themselves on their good taste could also obtain a great deal of pleasure by criticising the taste of others, as we see in some passages below.

From the time when he was fifteen or sixteen, he had planted a prunus tree in his courtyard, which he would prune and train morning and evening. Now the branches have spread out laterally to form a pavilion, under which five or six banquet tables can be set. In spring it is covered with myriads of blossoms, from which emanates a perfume that fills the air. Every morning the old man would take his staff and sit under the tree, keeping the birds off it. In the flowering season he would open his gate and let visitors in to enjoy themselves. If any gentlemen of culture came, the old man would provide choice tea and wine, and entertain them unstintingly all day long.

—Li Rihua, Diary from the Water-tasting Gallery, $9^{th}$ day of $2^{nd}$ month, 1614

Li Rihua (1565 – 1635), a painter of landscape, calligrapher and art critic in the Ming dynasty.

▶ Elderly gentlemen take their caged birds out in the early morning to sing in the fresh air among fragrant blossom.

▲ A view, in what is now Beihai Park in Beijing, from the pavilion known as "Between Hao and Pu" over an elegant marble bridge towards the gateway to this section of the park. The name of the building alludes to two stories from the "Autumn Floods" chapter of the Taoist classic *Zhuangzi*: the Hao River was the site of the debate between the philosophers Zhuangzi and Huizi as to whether one can know what fish enjoy, and Zhuangzi was fishing in the Pu River when he refused an invitation to govern the kingdom of Chu, saying that he preferred to be "a live tortoise dragging its tail in the mud."

On a winding path just within the gate, the first thing to be revealed is "An Urban Forest." A waterside enclosure overlooking a pond is bound to be called "Sky Light and Cloud Shadows." If it is "Thoughts of Hao and Pu" you usually see a fish-pond. If it is "Water and Bamboo Lodging" they are bound to have put in a bank of bamboo.

—Xie Zhaozhe, *Five Miscellaneous Offerings*

Xie Zhaozhe (1567 – 1624), from Fujian, was a senior Ming official who became an expert on irrigation and water control, and took a more general interest in geography and land management. His *Five Miscellaneous Offerings* covers an encyclopaedic range of information. Here he is criticising unimaginative and "tasteless" garden names.

*Qi records in his diary for the 7th day of the 2nd lunar month of 1637 that there were so many ladies visiting his garden that he had to take refuge in the nearby Buddhist hermitage. He wrote this poem on the occasion.*

Girls of eighteen with trailing silk sashes
Leave scented footprints at every step in the soil of the embankment.
A flock of mandarin-ducks calling and crying to one another,
Aunt holds hands with the new bride, older sister with younger.
Their breath forms an orchid fragrance which disperses into clouds;
A warm breeze ruffles into crepe their Xiang River skirts.
Stooping towards the ripples they view the reflections of their rosy faces,
Leaning down over fallen blossoms like swooping swallows.
Among thickets of greenery around lofty pines and ancient rocks,
A sudden glimpse of a thousand, no, a myriad buds of red.
From their snake-coil hairdos bound with oriole-tail bandeaus

Comes a gentle sound as their jewelled hair-ornaments
tinkle.
Among the bamboo and through the flowers they
cross the little bridge;
Moving and pausing on an upper storey they wave
their slender hands.
As the winding path takes a sudden turn they raise
their gauzy hems,
Lips slightly parted in a smile as if about to speak.
They block the ways with their colourful jackets and
hats,
So that one is forced to slip aside into the Bay of
Concealed Spring.
The lads point out how fine their new outfits are,
And mistake them for Su Xiaoxiao from the houses of
pleasure.
A rider's whip drops as he halts his black stallion
bridled with jade;
A look full of emotion from amid powder and rouge
steals out to meet his.
The intoxicating complexion of a fine flower will enter
his dreams:
Oh to be a pair of butterflies fluttering at the
branches' tips!

—Qi Biaojia, *Ladies on a Spring Outing to Allegory Mountain*

▲ Here, more of Du Jin's imperial concubines (see page 10) are enjoying themselves in a garden: the group on the left are playing "keepy-uppy" with a football (a popular sport for both men and women in imperial

China), while on the right of the central Taihu rock another group are looking out over a pond shaded by a willow tree.

My dear Qi,

Of the difficulties of creating a garden, one is the difficulty of construction, but a greater difficulty is that of naming. If the names are too vulgar then that's no good, but if they are too cultured then they are not remarkable... Zhang Zhongshan wanted to take a burning brand to the four-character horizontal signboards and the vertical matching couplets which are stuck all over the beams and columns of the Pavilion in the Heart of the Lake on the West Lake [in Hangzhou] to get rid of their bad karma... The scenic features of your Allegory Mountain which have been named amount to forty-nine sites, and not one character even borders on vulgarity. It is extremely difficult to reach this level. But if you command me to compose matching poems for each name, they will be crude and inadequate... Must dash; can't say all I want. Yours, Zhang Dai.

—Zhang Dai, *Letter to Qi Biaojia*

Zhang Dai (1597 – after 1679) was a member of one of the most distinguished families in Shaoxing in the late Ming dynasty, and a close friend of Qi Biaojia's cousin, as well as being on friendly terms with Qi himself; both men were enthusiastic patrons of the theatre.

▲ Calligraphic inscriptions in the Artless Administrator's Garden, Suzhou. The couplet reads: Rivers and hills seem to await the visitor, flowers and willows generously bestow their beauty. The horizontal plaque above the window gives the name of the building: "With whom shall I sit?" Gallery. The name comes from a lyric poem (*ci*) by the great poet Su Shi (Su Dongpo, 1037 – 1101), in which he asks "With whom shall I sit?" and answers "The bright moon, the clear breeze, and myself." Visitors to the "With whom shall I sit?" Gallery are left to find the answer by themselves: such puzzles set by the names of garden features are part of the fun of a garden visit.

In the case of artificial mountains in Suzhou, in addition to the complete provision of rocks and earth, a skilled craftsman is employed to construct them. As to the expenses for transport and construction, one cannot get away with less than one thousand taels. But in the degree of skill or lack of it in construction, what is as good as skill? Everything is perfectly finished; scenes are not repeated; rocks are not placed back to front; the degree of sparseness or denseness is appropriate; high and low are harmoniously disposed. In the midst of human artifice, the natural is not missing; a confined space still holds a sense of the wilderness. It should not be so fussy as to be tiresome; it should not be so regular as to approach vulgarity; it should not be exaggerated and striving after magnificence; it should not be so very elaborate as to lose its truth to nature. This is the way to let people wander and relax in it from one year's end to the next without growing bored.

—Xie Zhaozhe, *Five Miscellaneous Offerings*

▲ The Ge Yuan or Bamboo Garden in Yangzhou, created in the 19th century, is famous for its four scenic areas representing each of the four seasons by means of different rockery arrangements. Here we see the "summer" area, in which delicate, foraminous Taihu rocks are used to suggest vapour drifting up from the surface of the pool in the summer heat and to form grottos in which visitors could enjoy the cool atmosphere.

# Feasting and Drinking

One of the great garden pleasures was to use the garden as a setting for banquets and drinking parties. The numerous garden buildings meant that these occasions were unaffected by the weather.

◀ This decorative jar, which may have been used as a wine-vessel, shows a scene of officials banqueting in a garden setting, with musicians playing for their entertainment. There is a painted screen behind the table to shelter them from any wind. The chrysanthemums around the neck of the jar suggest that the season is autumn. On the lid, children play around a garden rockery.

Meeting in this garden fragrant with peach blossom, we enjoy the pleasures of family relationships. My younger relatives are handsome and talented, every one of them a Xie Huilian; but as I chant my poems, I am the one to feel inferior to Xie Lingyun. Our enjoyment of this secluded place is infinite; our elevated conversation reflects our pure ideals. A marvellous feast is spread for us to sit among the flowers, we set our winged goblets floating to grow drunk beneath the moon. If we have no fine verses, how can we express the refinement of our hearts? Those who fail to complete a poem will be sconced three cups, just as at that historic banquet in the Golden Valley.

—Li Bai, *Evening Banquet in Spring in Garden of Peaches and Plums*

Li Bai (701 – 762), great Tang poet.

▶ *Li Bai's Evening Banquet in Spring in the Garden of Peaches and Plums* (detail)
Qing dynasty
Silk tapestry
Height 136 cm, width 70.8 cm
Liaoning Provincial Museum

After lunch we went off to the South Garden, carrying cushions and mats with us. We picked a place in the shade of a willow tree and sat down. First we made tea, and when we had finished it we warmed the wine and cooked the food. The wind and sun were exquisite. The earth was golden, and the blue clothes and red sleeves of strollers filled the paths between the fields, while butterflies and bees flew all around us. The scene was so intoxicating one hardly needed to drink.

—Shen Fu, *Six Records of a Floating Life*; translation by Leonard Pratt & Chiang Su-hui, Penguin Books, 1983

Although Shen Fu (1763 – ?1810) failed at almost everything to which he turned his hand in life, his beautifully written autobiography, *Six Records of a Floating Life*, has brought posthumous fame to him and his beloved wife Yun.

◀ Gu Silk Embroidery of *A Lake with Rocks, Flowers and Butterflies*
Han Ximeng (active early 17th century), late Ming period
Height 30.3 cm, width 23.9 cm
Shanghai Museum

This exquisite silk embroidery shows butterflies fluttering around dianthus flowers in a garden with a delicate Taihu rock—a scene that would have delighted Shen Fu and his wife Yun.

While at Haining I once went to visit the Chen family's Garden of Peaceful Waves, which occupied twenty acres of land and which was covered with towers and pavilions, winding lanes and galleries. With the birds twittering and the petals dropping to the ground, it was like being deep in the mountains. Of all the artificial rock gardens I have seen that were built on flat ground, this one looked the most natural.

Once we gave a dinner at the Cassia Tower there, and you could not smell the food for the scent of the flowers. Only the smell of the pickled ginger was not overcome, but then ginger and cassia both turn more pungent with age, like loyal ministers who are made of strong stuff.

—Shen Fu, *Six Records of a Floating Life*; translation by Leonard Pratt & Chiang Su-hui, Penguin Books, 1983

▶ *Drinking Together under the Pines*
Tang Di (1286 – 1364), Yuan dynasty
Hanging scroll, ink and colour on silk
Height 141.1 cm, width 97.1 cm
Shanghai Museum

# Water and Tea Tasting

As well as being skilled in wine-tasting, Chinese connoisseurs enjoyed practising their expertise in tasting tea, and even in appreciating the subtle flavours of pure water from different sources.

◀ Outdoor terrace of the teahouse at the Leaping Tiger Spring near Hangzhou. The water from this spring, often called "the third great spring under heaven," has long been appreciated by connoisseurs, who regard it as particularly suited to the flavour of the local "Dragon Well" tea.

When lotus flowers bloom in the summer, they close up at night but open again in the morning. [My wife] Yun used to put a few tea-leaves in a gauze bag and put it inside a lotus flower before it closed in the evening. The next morning she would take out the tea and boil it with natural spring water. It had a wonderful and unique fragrance.

—Shen Fu, *Six Records of a Floating Life*; translation by Leonard Pratt & Chiang Su-hui, Penguin Books, 1983

▲ Large carved red lacquer dish with two mandarin ducks on a lotus pond
Ming, Yongle reign period (1403 – 1424)
Height 4.2 cm, diameter 32.4 cm, base diameter 25.1 cm
Liaoning Provincial Museum

Of celestial springs [rain water], autumn water is the best, and next best is water in the plum-rain season [late spring – early summer]. Autumn water is pale and chill; plum-rain water is pale and sweet. Of spring and winter waters, spring is better than winter, no doubt because of the temperate winds and gentle rain, while the stormy rain of the summer months is unsuitable: perhaps because of the activity of the wind and thunder dragons, it is most apt to make people ill. To collect the water one should use a cloth suspended in the centre of the courtyard; water dripping from the eaves cannot be used.

—Wen Zhenheng, *A Treatise on Superfluous Things*

▶ *Deep Autumn on Mount Hua* (detail)
Lan Ying (1585 – ?)
Ming dynasty
Hanging scroll, ink and colour on silk
Height 310.9 cm, width 102.2 cm
Shanghai Museum

▲ This painting by Wen Zhengming records a meeting of friends to taste the water of the Huishan spring near Wuxi, which was highly regarded by connoisseurs. Two gentlemen are already sitting by the wellhead, under a thatched pavilion, while other friends are just arriving.

Slow-flowing natural springs like the Huishan spring are the best, and the next choice is a spring which is clear and cold [this refers to the property of "coldness" in Chinese medicine, rather than the temperature]. It is not enough for a spring to be clear, but it is hard to find a cold one: one with a lot of soil, slimy sand and coagulated mud will certainly not be clear or cold. Some springs are fragrant and sweet, but sweetness is easy to find while fragrance is hard; there is no known case of a spring which is fragrant without being sweet. Do not consume water from rushing waterfalls or swirling rapids; if consumed over any length of time it will cause migraine. Waterfalls like the Water Curtain on Mount Lu or the one on Mount Tiantai are all very well to look at and listen to, but they do not qualify as vintage waters; hot springs produce sulphur and are also not potable.

—Wen Zhenheng, *A Treatise on Superfluous Things*

▶

*The Qianlong Emperor Examining a Painting*
Giuseppe Castiglione
(1688 – 1766)
Qing dynasty
Ink and colour on silk
Height 136.4 cm,
width 62 cm

This painting shows the Qianlong Emperor in a garden, dressed as a Chinese scholar in Ming costume, and engaged with two of the canonical literati pursuits: attendants in the foreground hold a zither, while a painting is being presented for his appreciation; various *objets d'art* are also arranged on the table beside him. The painting being shown to the Emperor depicts a Buddhist subject, the washing of the white elephant ridden by the Bodhisattva Samantabhadra.

# Literati Pursuits

The four activities traditionally considered characteristic of the educated class were "playing the zither, playing chess, writing calligraphy and appreciating paintings" (*qin qi shu hua*). These are often shown being pursued in a garden setting.

Chess or *weiqi* ("encirclement chess," better known in English by its Japanese name of *go*) was considered not only to provide training in military strategy but to bring its players closer to the immortals, who were thought to spend much of their infinite time playing chess. A well-known legend told of a wood-cutter who came upon chess-players on a remote mountain. He laid down his axe to watch them play, and when the game was over and he went to pick it up again, he found that so much time had passed in the mortal world that the handle of the axe had rotted away.

A social activity which was often enjoyed by the literati in their gardens was to float wine-cups along a meander—either a naturally winding stream or a channel specially cut in stone—while the participants sat alongside the watercourse. As a cup reached a participant, he had to compose a poetic couplet in sequence with that of the preceding player; if he failed to do so successfully, he was obliged to drink the contents of the cup. The occasion which gave rise to this pastime was a celebrated literary gathering in 353 at the Orchid Pavilion near Shaoxing, commemorated in a famous essay by the great calligrapher Wang Xizhi.

▶ *People and Activities: Appreciating Antiques in a Bamboo Grove* (detail)
Qiu Ying
Ming dynasty
Ink and colour on silk
Height 41.4 cm, width 33.8 cm

Sheltered from the breeze by two large painted screens, three gentlemen are examining paintings and antiques. Behind the screen a servant is fanning a stove to make tea, and among the bamboos in the background another pageboy lays out a chessboard on a stone table. Qiu Ying was a professional painter noted for his landscapes and scenes of literati life.

▲ After *Wangchuan Villa*, by Wang Wei, Tang Dynasty
Wang Wei (701 – 761) was one of the greatest poets and painters of the Tang dynasty. No original paintings from his hand survive, but his *Wangchuan Villa* is known from a number of later copies. Wangchuan Villa was the artist's own estate near the Tang capital Chang'an (present-day Xi'an). He also wrote many poems about the scenery of the estate, which reflect his profound Buddhist beliefs.

On the seventh day of the second month (c. 1600), when the weather had just cleared up, I climbed Master Gao's tower (a garden building) to gaze upon the snow upon the mountains. My host produced a copy of the "Wangchuan Villa" by

Guo Zhongshu (910 – 977), and an "Illustration to the Odes of Lu and Shang" by Ma Hezhi (active twelfth century) to show me. Both were pieces I had been hoping to appreciate all my life, and my heart and eyes were both delighted to an unspeakable degree. When I left him, I made this note in recognition of a rare experience in connoisseurship.

—The writer Feng Mengzhen (1546 – 1605) pays a visit to the connoisseur Gao Lian (fl. 1581 – 1591); translation by Craig Clunas, *Superfluous Things*, University of Illinois Press, 1991, p.16

## Chess-Board Rock

It takes a thousand years to complete a single game:
Victory and defeat are totally meaningless.
I would like to ask if by means of this game
Sacred and profane can perhaps communicate.

—Zhu Zhifan, *110 Poems on Scenes from the Garden of Sitting in Reclusion*

Zhu Zhifan (1564 – after 1624) was the highest-ranked graduate in the imperial examinations of 1595, and went on to be a successful official. A skilled calligrapher, he became well-known in Korea after going on an official mission there; paid in Korean sable furs and ginseng for his calligraphy, he was able to build up an outstanding art collection by selling these valuable items.

▶ *An Appointment to Play Chess in the Mountains* (detail)
Yuan dynasty
Ink and colour on silk
Height 106.5 cm, width 54 cm
Liaoning Provincial Museum

Playing chess is an important part of a hermit's life in the mountains, putting the players in touch with the immortals who are believed to live there. Life in a garden is a substitute for withdrawing to the mountains like the inhabitants of this scene.

▲ Blue and white *guan* jar with illustrations of the four accomplishments: music, chess, calligraphy and painting
Ming, Xuande reign period (1426 – 1435)
Diameter of mouth 22.1 cm, diameter of base 21.8 cm, height 34.4 cm

Unusually, the figures shown participating in the scholarly activities on this jar are women.

Playing chess is a way to pass one's leisure time, but it is not what you would call fun; playing the *qin* is certainly good for one's spiritual development, but it is hardly the way to have a good time. That is because to play the *qin* one should be properly dressed and formally seated, while playing chess requires attention to the rules of the chequered board. When all the chess pieces are set out, what further need is there for yet more formality? At a time when you are supposed to have banished all worries from your mind, what is the point of having to worry about winning or losing? Some people are quite prepared to give up official honours, fame and fortune, but when engaged in a competitive chess-match, they will let not a single move go unchallenged: this lack of a sense of proportion is just like selling one's birthright for a mess of pottage.

—Li Yu, "Listening to the *Qin* and Watching Chess" from *Random Notes on Idle Feelings*

So it is better to enjoy listening to the *qin* than to enjoy playing it, and better to be good at watching chess than to be good at competing. If somebody wins, I can be delighted on his behalf, but it's no skin off my nose if he loses, so I'm always on the winning side; if someone plays a harmonious melody, I benefit from the auspicious atmosphere, but if he makes a dreadful cacophony, it won't have any ill effect on me, so fortune always smiles on me. Sometimes, after watching or listening, you feel an urge to have a go yourself; it does no harm to do so occasionally, but by not spending your every moment immersed in it to the point that you cannot extricate yourself, that's the way to be a successful player of *qin* or chess.

—Li Yu, "Listening to the *Qin* and Watching Chess" from *Random Notes on Idle Feelings*

▶ *Sounds of the* Qin *in a Water Pavilion by Qiu Ying* (detail)
Silk tapestry
Ming dynasty
Length 138 cm, width 55.4 cm
Liaoning Provincial Museum

In the 9th year of the Yonghe period, a *kuichou* year (353), at the beginning of the last month of spring, there was a gathering at the Orchid Pavilion at Shanyin in Guiji, to celebrate the Festival of Purification. A great mass of worthies assembled, young and old all gathered together. The region has high mountains and steep ridges, flourishing woods and tall bamboo, as well as clear streams with swirling eddies, reflecting and setting each other off on either hand. A serpentine channel had been constructed on which to float goblets, and we sat in order beside it. Although there was no splendid clamour of pipes and strings, a goblet and a verse were enough to express our inner feelings.

▲ *Purification Ceremony at the Orchid Pavilion*
Wen Zhengming
Ming dynasty
Handscroll, ink and colour on paper
Height 20.8 cm, width 77.8 cm
Palace Museum, Beijing

On this day, the sky was bright, the air was clear, and a kindly breeze blew gently; looking up, we could contemplate the vastness of the universe, and looking down, we could perceive the variety of the forms of creation. Thus by looking around and expressing our emotions, we could attain the greatest pleasures of sight and hearing. It was truly pleasurable.

—Wang Xizhi (307? – 365?), *Preface to the Orchid Pavilion Anthology*

*A description in the great eighteenth-century novel* The Story of the Stone *(also known as* A Dream of Red Mansions*) of a poetry competition which takes place in the garden of the family's mansion gives a good idea of how these social activities were organised:*

"As I was on my way here just now," said Li Wan, "I saw them carrying in two pots of white crab-blossom. It was so pretty. Couldn't you have white crab-blossom for your subject?"

"We haven't all seen it yet," said Ying-chun. "How are they going to write poems about it if they haven't seen it?"

"We all know what white crab-blossom looks like," said Bao-chai. "I don't see why we necessarily have to look at it in order to be able to write a poem about it..." "Very well, then, I'll set your rhymes," said Ying-chun.

...She ...turned to a little maid who was leaning in the doorway looking on.

"Give us a word," she said. "Any word."

"Door," said the girl.

"That means the first line must end with 'door'," said Ying-chun. She turned again to the girl: "Another one."

"Pot," said the girl.

"Right, 'pot'," said Ying-chun, and going over to a little nest of drawers in which rhyme-cards were kept, she pulled out one of them and asked the maid to select two cards from it at random. These turned out to be the cards for "not" and "spot."

"Now," she said to the girl, "pick any card out of any drawer. Just one."

The girl pulled out another drawer and picked out the card for "day."

"All right," said Ying-chun. "That means that your first line must end in "door," your second in "pot," your fourth in "not," your sixth in "spot," and the rhyming couplet in the seventh and eighth lines must end in 'day'."

—Cao Xueqin, *The Story of the Stone*, Chapter 37; translation by David Hawkes, Penguin Books

*On the following spread*

▶ From the illustrations of *Dream of Red Mansions*
Sun Wen
Qing dynasty
Lüshun Museum

▲ *Wu Yangzi in Meditation*
Tang Yin
Ming dynasty
Handscroll, ink on paper
Length 29.5 cm, width 103.5 cm

Tang Yin (1470 – 1523) was one of several noted painters in mid-Ming Suzhou. A romantic character, he was almost as celebrated for his love affairs and fondness for wine as he was for his art.

When dawn came, the mountain peak was fringed
with faint cloud;
Suddenly, as I look, the sky is dark and tinged
with a sunset glow.
Seated in meditation on my prayer-mat I utter not
a word,
But the single sound of a clear chime is heard by
the gathered mountains.

—Qi Biaojia, *Miscellaneous Impressions of Allegory Mountain at the Qingming Festival IV*

# Drama

As well as poetry composition and recital, drama performances were also staged in gardens. Many wealthy families had their own drama troupes to perform for them at family parties and on festive occasions. Sometimes a garden also formed the setting for the action of the drama, as in the case of the much-loved sixteenth-century play *The Peony Pavilion* by the great playwright Tang Xianzu (1550 – 1616).

◀ The He Family Garden in Yangzhou, constructed in the 19th century, has a purpose-built stage located on the central pond. Here the family and their friends could enjoy private theatrical performances, the men seated around the pond and the women watching from the balconies of their upper-floor apartments. The water surrounding the stage allows the singing to be heard more clearly by the audience. Many private residences in the Qing dynasty had their own theatre buildings.

[Du Liniang speaks] If one did not come to the garden grove, how would one know what spring was like?

[Aria to the tune *Black Gauze Robe*]

In fact enticing purple and charming red flowers are bursting out all over;

Lovely as they are, they grow beside a blocked well and tumbled-down wall.

Such a fine day, such lovely scenery; what is to be done?

Whose is the garden in which we enjoy ourselves?

[Speaks] Why have my father and mother never mentioned such a fine sight?

—Tang Xianzu, "Wandering in the Garden" from *The Peony Pavilion*

Tang Xianzu (1550 – 1616) was the greatest playwright of the Ming dynasty. A number of his plays survive, but *The Peony Pavilion* is by far the most popular, and still frequently performed.

▲ A painting from the Long Gallery in the Summer Palace shows the love-lorn heroine of *The Peony Pavilion*, Du Liniang, visiting the garden with her maid. The plum blossom alludes to Du Liniang's dream lover, Liu Mengmei, whose name means "Dreaming of Plum Blossom." They meet in Du Liniang's dream after her first visit to the garden.

[Duet sung by Du Liniang and her maid Spring Fragrance]
In the morning they float up and in the evening coil themselves away,
The clouds and vapours around the emerald pavilion.
Threads of rain and snatches of breeze,
Misty waves and a painted boat.
A lady behind a brocade screen would be wrong to despise this spring scene.
[Spring Fragrance speaks] All the flowers are out, but it is still too early for the peonies.
[Du Liniang: aria to the tune *Dear Sister*]
Throughout the green hills the nightjar has sung the azaleas red;
Beyond the roseleaf raspberry, misty fronds wave in drunken softness.
Oh, Spring Fragrance, although peonies are fine, how could they come before the passing of spring?
[Spring Fragrance speaks] The orioles and swallows are all in pairs.
[Duet]

Idly we gaze: every twitter of the swallows' voices
is sharply clear;
Every warble of the orioles' song is roundly liquid.
[Du Liniang speaks] Let's go.
[Spring Fragrance speaks] You could never get
your fill of looking at this garden.
[Du Liniang speaks] Why speak of it? [They
leave.]

—Tang Xianzu, "Wandering in the Garden" from *The Peony Pavilion*

*On the following spread*

▶ A performance of the much-loved Kunqu opera *The Peony Pavilion* staged in June 2010 in the Kezhi Garden in Shanghai's Qingpu county; the garden itself formed the stage set, and the audience was seated around the pond, the water naturally amplifying the sound.

# Boating and Fishing

Many gardens had ponds large enough to take a small boat, in which the owner could float with a fishing rod and imagine himself as a simple fisherman, free from the cares of official life. He could recall the philosopher Zhuangzi, who preferred to continue fishing by the River Pu rather than answer the summons to take up a government position, or the fisherman who rowed upstream to discover the idyllic world of the Peach Blossom Spring in the well-known narrative and poem by the pastoral poet Tao Yuanming. On a more practical level, the fish in a garden pond would also provide a source of protein for the family's meals.

◀ Boating is still a much-enjoyed pastime in the parks of modern-day China. Here, the Kunming Lake in the Summer Palace outside Beijing is dotted with small pleasure-craft, allowing people to enjoy the cool air of the lake in the summer heat. The pagoda on Jade Spring Hill can be seen in the distance.

A skiff may be ten feet or more long, and about three feet wide, and may be launched on a pond, or sometimes propelled by a single oar along a stream or river, or else moored by a winding bank in the shade of willows, where you can flex your rod and bait your hook, or enjoy the moonlight and sing with the breeze. You can have an awning made of blue cloth with shades at either side and two bamboo poles to prop up the awning at the bow, while it is tied to two rings at the stern, where a servant will stand to row it.

—Wen Zhenheng, *A Treatise on Superfluous Things*

▶ *Wang Huizhi Visiting Dai Andao on a Snowy Night*
Zhang Wo
Yuan dynasty
Hanging scroll, ink on paper
Height 91.1 cm, width 39.3 cm
Shanghai Museum

This painting depicts a well-known story from a 5th-century collection of anecdotes about famous people. Wang Huizhi goes to visit his friend Dai Andao, but returns without entering Dai's house. Asked why, he explains, "I set off because I felt like it, and when I no longer felt like it I came back; what need was there to see Dai?"

錢塘王氏
潔軒珍藏

Turtle-Fishing Terrace

My thoughts range beyond the hanging line;
My pure heart goes toward the source of the water.
Letting my gaze roam beyond the end of the terrace,
I seem to catch a glimpse of a fishing village.

— Zhu Zhifan, "Poems on Scenes" from the *Garden of Sitting in Reclusion*

▲ *Yellow Mountain Thatched Hall*
Yu Zhiding
Qing dynasty
Handscroll, ink and colour on paper
Height 40.3 cm, length 131.8 cm

By a garden pond surrounded by rocks, trees and pavilions, a gentleman sits with a fishing rod, but his body is half turned away from the main part of the pond, and he does not seem to mind very much whether he catches any fish or not. Yu Zhiding (1647 – c.1709) was known as a portraitist as well as a painter of landscapes and other subjects; the painting, dated 1702, is a portrait of Tian Guangyun, from Taizhou, near Yangzhou, and the painted garden presumably bears some similarity to Tian's real garden.

## Mirror Boat

Water so clean that suddenly it seems to have no
substance:
The pale pike seem to be swimming in the void.
If you bend down to look you can see the spring
birds,
Twisting and turning among the waterweed.

—Ruan Dacheng, *Miscellaneous Songs on Garden Living*

Ruan Dacheng (1587 – 1646) was a poet, playwright and politician of the late Ming dynasty. An enthusiastic garden owner, he was a patron of the garden designer Ji Cheng, and sponsored the publication of his great work on garden design, *The Craft of Gardens*. This poem is one of a series which Ruan wrote about various features in one of his own gardens, the Assembly Garden, which was located in or near Nanjing.

◄ Enamelled jar with fish and waterweed design
Qing, Kangxi reign period (1662 – 1722)
Diameter of mouth 6.4 cm, diameter of base 6 cm, height 22.1 cm
Shanghai Museum

# Festivals

Gardens provided a wonderful setting for all kinds of celebrations, from birthdays and other personal occasions to the great festivals of the Chinese calendar. On these festivals, it was customary for wealthy families to open parts of their private gardens to the public, who would have a rare opportunity to see how the other half lived and be able to enjoy lantern displays or sometimes theatrical or musical performances.

The Lantern Festival, which took place on the first full moon of the lunar new year, enabled wealthy families to display their gardens and the splendour of their decorative lanterns, and for the less wealthy to enjoy the brilliant scene.

◀ *Shared Enjoyment at the Lantern Festival*
Guan Xining (1712 – 1785)
Qing dynasty

The Lantern Festival is being celebrated in the garden of a wealthy family. Mother and Father are seated at the centre of the scene, in front of a large rockery, watching their children play around them. Some hold lanterns, others seem to be fighting a battle, with flags denoting the different "armies."

In the *xinchou* year of Wanli [1601], my father and his brothers held a lantern exhibition on Dragon Mountain, with a hundred frames made of split wood, painted with red varnish, garlanded with patterned brocade, and with lanterns hung in threes. There were lanterns not only on the frames, and not only along the stepped path, but all over the mountain and along the valley, every branch, every twig had its lantern, and from the gate of the city god's temple, all up and down Penglai Ridge, everywhere had its lantern. Looking down from the mountain it looked like a river of stars flowing downwards, coiling and eddying.... Lantern enthusiasts bought wine and sat on mats on the ground up and down the mountain. Nowhere on the mountain was without its lanterns, no lantern was without a picnic mat, no picnic mat lacked picnickers, and everyone was singing or playing music. The men and women who came to look at the lanterns, as soon as they entered the temple gate, could hardly move their heads or feet to look or turn around, and could only be swept along, up or down hill, with the movement of the crowd, with no idea where they were going, and no choice but to follow.... There was a story that on the night of the fifteenth, as the lanterns dimmed and people dispersed, while the cooks were collecting up their dishes and remnants, six or seven beautiful women bought wine, and when they had finished, there was one of them who had still not opened a flask. She bought a large jar of at least four quarts in volume, and produced melon seeds from her pockets, and in an instant had emptied the jar and disappeared. People thought she must be a star-woman, or possibly the wine star. And another thing: there was a ne'er-do-well who had occupied an empty building of several rooms to the left of the city god's temple and filled it up with pretty boys, calling it "Curtain Alley." That night, a handsome young man came and made advances to one of the boys, snuffing the candles, getting completely drunk, and acting most indecently, but when his shirt came undone, "he" turned out to be a woman; she left before it was light, and no-one knew where she came from or who she was: perhaps she was the incarnation of a fox-spirit.

—Zhang Dai, "Lanterns on Dragon Mountain" from *Dream Memories of Joyous Hermitage*

▶ Lantern Festival celebrations are far from being a thing of the past. Here the festival is being celebrated around the teahouse beside the Yu Garden in Shanghai, with lanterns strung from the eaves of the teahouse and hung along the balustrade of the Nine-Bend Bridge.

There is nothing worth looking at on the West Lake in mid-August, except the mid-August people.

Observation shows that these mid-August people are divided into five categories. The first category consists of people who ride on lofty barges with complete orchestras playing, holding official banquets in their full regalia, surrounded by a throng of servants and illuminations. So dazzling are the noise and lights that although these people are nominally there to look at the moon, they never actually look at it.

The second category ride in equally lofty barges, with the most distinguished female companions, and accompanied by handsome young pages. In a hubbub of giggles and exclamations they sit on the open decks gazing to left and right; but although they are sitting in the moonlight they never actually look at the moon.

The third category also ride in barges, accompanied by music and singing; these are fashionable courtesans and notable priests. They drink in a restrained manner and sing in low tones to the music of gentle flutes and lightly plucked guitars, singing and playing in harmony. They too are sitting in the moonlight, and hoping that everyone else is appreciating how much they are appreciating the moonlight.

Yet another category doesn't bother with boats or carriages, or indeed formal dress or hats; instead they stuff themselves with food and drink and yell for a bunch of friends to join them, shoving through the throngs of sightseers at Zhaoqing Monastery or the Broken Bridge, bawling and shouting, acting much drunker than they really are, and singing tunelessly. They are looking at the moon too, and looking at the people who are looking at the moon, and looking at the people who aren't looking at the moon, but not actually noticing anything at all.

The last category ride in small boats, in casual dress, with a neat table and a warm stove on which to boil water for their tea. They quietly pass their drinks around in simple cups. A group of close friends and elegant women, they invite the moon to join their party, either in the shadow of the trees, or away from the crowds, on the Inner Lake. Although they are looking at the moon, other people don't notice them looking at it, nor do they make a great performance of doing so....

—Zhang Dai, "Mid-August on the West Lake" from *Dream Memories of Joyous Hermitage*

Autumn colours tint the trees around the West Lake in Hangzhou.

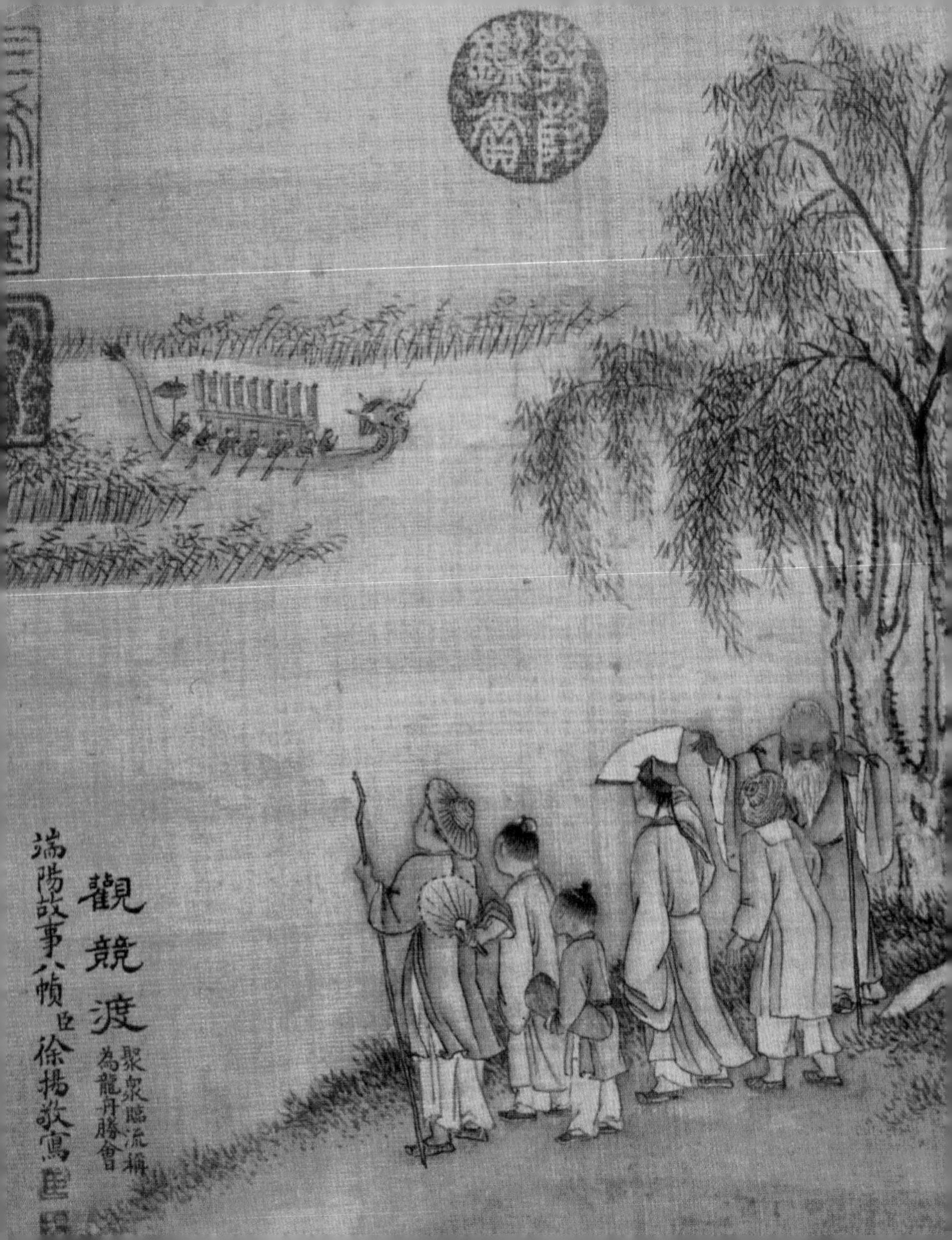

觀競渡
聚泉臨流稱
為龍舟勝會
端陽故事八幀臣徐揚敬寫

On the fifth day of the fifth month the skies are clear and bright;
Willow flowers drift over the river while orioles hymn the dawn.
From the ladies' silk dresses on either bank, fragrance assails
one's nostrils;
Silver hair-clasps glitter in the sunlight like frosty sword-blades.
The drums sound thrice and the scarlet flag is raised;
Two dragons leap forward, racing over the waves.
The blades' shadows slice the waves like a myriad whirling swords;
The drum-beats strike the billows like a thousand rolls of thunder.
The foremost boat, pushing through the water, has already
reached the finish;
The hindmost boat, losing momentum, is vainly beating the air.

—Zhang Jianfeng, *Song of the Dragon Boat Race*

Zhang Jianfeng (735 – 800) was a high-ranking Tang dynasty military official.

◀ This painting is the last leaf of an album of eight scenes of the Dragon Boat (Duanwu) Festival. A mixed group of people, an elderly man, a young scholar with attendants, and farmers in straw hats, are watching the progress of a dragon boat on the river. Xu Yang was an 18th-century artist from Suzhou, specialising in topographical scenes, who became a court painter to the Qianlong Emperor.

# Plants and Animals

For some people, at least, the cultivation of plants was one of the great garden pleasures, although many more were able to appreciate the flowers they produced. Birdsong was also much appreciated, as was the presence of animals, particularly deer, which were associated with Taoist immortals.

◀ Golden carp swarm in the waters of Suzhou's Garden for Lingering (Liu Yuan)

Jin Rusheng is fond of cultivating plants. There was an empty plot in front of his house, bordered by a small stream. Beside the stream Rusheng built a small gallery of three bays, and along the area to the north, which was long rather than square, he set a bamboo fence to the left. To the north where it bordered on the street, he built an earthen wall, with a decorative trellis just inside the wall to cover its foot. In front of that he placed a stone balustrade more than ten feet long and quite narrow. In front of the balustrade he erected a "mountain" of Snail Hill rocks with several twists and turns, to great artistic effect. He had more than a hundred flowering trees, planted hapharzardly, here dense, there sparse, with a fine sense of composition. … Rusheng's constitution is weak and he is liable to illness, but he gets up early and before he has even washed his face or combed his hair, he is to be found prostrate on the ground catching pests; despite the vast number of his plants, he inspects the roots and the underside of the leaves of each one of them at least once a day.

… He insists on attending to everything himself, and does not care even when frosts chaps his hands or sun burns his face. The God of Vegetation is pleased with his efforts, so three *lingzhi* fungus have recently grown as an auspicious sign to bless him.

—Zhang Dai, "The Plants of Jin Rusheng" from *Dream Memories of Joyous Hermitage*

*On page 107*

▶ *Chrysanthemum*
Sun Long (15th century)
Ming dynasty
Album leaf, ink and colour on silk
Height 22.9 cm, width 21.5 cm
Shanghai Museum

Mr Zhang of Yanzhou invited me to see his chrysanthemums, five *li* out of town. When I reached his garden, I wound my way through the entire area which he had turned into a garden, and then went right round the area which he had not yet finished turning into a garden, without seeing a single chrysanthemum, which I found strange. A little later, the proprietor led me to an open plot of waste land, with a three-bay shed made of reeds, and ushered me inside. As I looked around me, I could not call what I saw merely "chrysanthemums" but "a sea of chrysanthemums." Along three sides of the shed, he had built a three-tier stand with the chrysanthemum plants arranged in order of height. Their flowers were as large as ceramic bowls, each one spherical, each one covered with "scales," each one with gold- or silver-tinted petals like lotuses, of glorious colours, quite unlike ordinary varieties.

—Zhang Dai, "A Sea of Chrysanthemums" from *Dream Memories of Joyous Hermitage*

▲ *Flowers* (detail)
Yun Shouping
Qing dynasty
Album leaf, ink and colour on silk
Height 29.9 cm, width 22.2 cm
Shanghai Museum

Yun Shouping (1633 – 90), was a specialist in flower painting. He revived the "boneless" style of the Song dynasty (painting in colour without the use of an ink outline), and drew flowers from life, which was rather unusual in Chinese painting tradition.

One spends a whole year looking after plants for ten days of enjoyment when they flower... Abundant flowers and unspecified trees should be planted by the acre, while by the railings in one's courtyard one should have only ancient trunks with writhing branches, unusual varieties with recherché names, with leafy twigs pleasingly arranged, and all set at the appropriate distance. By rocky watersides, tree-trunks may slope and spread horizontally; they may form a forest as far as the eye can see, or there may be just a single stem in solitary splendour. Plants and trees should not be all mixed up together, but one should plant them in the right places, so that there is always something to look at throughout the four seasons, as though one were living within a painting.... As for cultivating orchids and planting chrysanthemums, their methods were known in the most ancient times; to use them from time to time in instructing one's gardeners and testing their professional knowledge is part of the duty of a recluse.

—Wen Zhenheng, *A Treatise on Superfluous Things*

▲ Bonsai trees displayed in a courtyard of the Lion Grove Garden in Suzhou.

In raising potted trees, first select those which have roots that are exposed and crooked like chickens' feet. Cut off about the first three branches, then let the others grow. Each branch should have a section of the trunk to itself, with from seven to nine branches to the top of the tree. There should not be two branches opposite one another like shoulders, nor should the joints be swollen like the knees of a crane. The branches should grow out in all directions, not only to the right and left, or to the front and back, otherwise the tree will look bare. Some trees are called "double-trunked" or "triple-trunked"; this is when two or three trees grow from the same roots. If the roots of a tree do not look like chickens' feet the tree will look unattractive, as if it has been just stuck in the dirt.

—Shen Fu, *Six Records of a Floating Life*; translation by Leonard Pratt & Chiang Su-hui, Penguin Books, 1983

Flowers and birds are two things created by Nature to delight the human race. Since attractive flowers with their tender petals can stand in for beautiful women, except for the drawback that they lack speech, the different types of birds were created to supplement them… However, worldly people don't understand this, but consider them as inanimate objects: wonderful flowers often pass before their view without their noticing, birds may sing delightfully without their hearing anything… It's quite a different story in my case. Whenever there is a day when flowers and willow-fronds compete in elegance, or the winged tribe challenge one another with the complexity of their song, I always give thanks to Heaven, the mighty artificer, and give the credit to creative Nature, making a libation from my drink and an offering from my food like a faithful Buddhist devotee.

—Li Yu, "Looking at Flowers and Listening to Birdsong" from *Random Notes of Idle Feelings*

▲ Enamelled *Doucai* dish with design of birds paying court to a phoenix
Qing, Kangxi reign period
Diameter of mouth 55.4 cm, diameter of base 32.1 cm, height 9.6 cm
Shanghai Museum

Songbirds which brush the rooftops as they fly low, frolicking fish which push aside the waterweed as they criss-cross the pond: these have a meeting of minds with the recluse, who can watch them all day without tiring. He observes their calls and their colours, their postures as they drink or peck: in the distance as they nest in trees or holes, roost on the sand or swim in the bays, soar in the broad empyrean or float on the bosom of the deep; close at hand as they flit through the room or greet the eaves—the magpie, harbinger of the year, the cock, watchman of the dawn, the oriole, vernal twitterer, the crow, evening croaker: too many species to enumerate.... In fact, training pet birds and enjoying the activities of ducks and fish forms part of the management of mountain forests [gardens].

—Wen Zhenheng, *A Treatise on Superfluous Things*

◀ *Flower and Bird*
Ming dynasty
Embroidery
Length 25.1 cm, width 23.7 cm
Liaoning Provincial Museum

If you raise deer they can roam freely about; if you breed fish they can be caught. In cool summer pavilions you can play drinking-games, mix ice with your drinks, and feel the breeze rising among the bamboos and trees. In warm winter apartments you can gather round the stove, and melt snow to make your tea while the water bubbles in the wine-warmer. Your troubles will be quenched along with your thirst. The night-rain patters on the plantain leaves like a mermaid's pearly tears. The dawn breeze soughs through the willows, as if caressing a dancing girl's slender waist. Transplant some bamboos in front of your window, and set aside some pear trees to form a courtyard. The scene is bathed in moonlight, the wind whispers. The moonlight plays quietly over lute and books, the wind ruffles a half-circle of autumn water. We feel a pure atmosphere around our table and seats; the common dust of the world is far from our souls.

—Ji Cheng, *The Craft of Gardens*

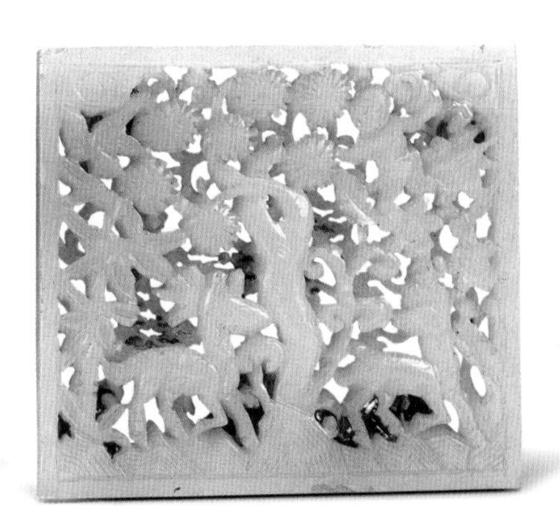

▲ Transparent white jade ornament carved with pine, deer and monkey
Ming dynasty
Length 6.8 cm, width 5.8 cm, thickness 0.85 cm
Liaoning Provincial Museum

▲ Autumn colours in the Summer Palace, Beijing

# The Four Seasons

The garden should provide interest and pleasure throughout the four seasons, each of which had its appropriate activities. Ji Cheng's *The Craft of Gardens* sums up the delights of each season.

Spring will embody the poem on "Living as a Hermit" by Pan Yue, or Qu Yuan's affection for the fragrant herbs. When sweeping your paths take care of the orchid shoots, and they will send their fragrance into your retreat. Roll up your blinds and greet the swallows who slice through the light breeze like shears. Everywhere float drifting petals and the drowsy threads of willows. If the cold still makes you shiver, hang up a high swing. You can enjoy yourself at leisure and delight in the hills and valleys. Your thoughts will travel beyond the confines of this world of dust, and you will feel as though you were wandering within a painting.

—Ji Cheng, *The Craft of Gardens*

▶ *Playing on a Swing by the Serpentine Pond in the Third Month*
Chen Mei
Qing dynasty

A painting from an album showing the pastimes of the Palace women through the twelve months of the year. Here, as spring arrives and the air warms, the women are enjoying being out of doors, playing on a swing among the spring blossom. Chen Mei was an 18th-century court painter.

From the summer shade of the woods the song of the oriole starts; in the folds of the hills you suddenly hear a wood-cutter singing and, as a breeze springs up from the cool of the forest, you feel as though you were transported back to the realm of the Emperor Fuxi. The hermit recites poetry in his pine-wood hut, and the gentleman of leisure plucks his lute in a grove of bamboo. The red garments of the lotuses are newly washed, and the green jade of the bamboos gently chimes. You can gaze at the bamboo by a bend in the stream, and watch the fish from the banks of the Hao. Mist drifts through the mountains, and the floating clouds sink down as you lean on the railing. Ripples cover the surface of the water, and you feel a cool breeze as you recline on your pillow.

—Ji Cheng, *The Craft of Gardens*

◀ The fragrance of lotuses is redolent of summer in the garden.

Your light summer clothes can no longer withstand the fresh chill of autumn, but the scent of the lotuses in the pond still draws you to them. The phoenix-tree leaves are startled into their autumn fall, and the insects cry, hidden in the grasses. The level surface of the lake is a boundless expanse of floating light; the outline of the hills is of delicious beauty. There comes into view a skein of white egrets, and rank upon rank of crimson maples flushed with wine. You gaze afar from a high terrace, rub your eyes and wonder at the clear sky; leaning over the void from a spacious pavilion, you raise your glass and hail the bright moon. Imperceptibly a heavenly fragrance steals around as the osmanthus seeds sadly fall.

—Ji Cheng, *The Craft of Gardens*

▶ A covered walkway is glimpsed through a screen of autumn leaves in the Ancient Garden of Elegance in Nanxiang, near Shanghai.

You notice that beside the withered hedge the chrysanthemum flowers are over; it is winter now, time to explore the warmer hillsides to see if the first plum blossoms are out. You should tie a little money to your staff and invite your rustic neighbours to a drink. The plum flower is like a lovely woman coming from the moonlit woods, while the gentleman of high ideals lies in his snow-covered cottage. The lowering clouds are wintry grey; the few leaves left on the trees rustle together. Wind-blown crows perch on some sparse trees in the setting sun; cold-driven geese utter a few cries under the waning moon. Waking from a dream by the window of his study, a solitary figure recites poetry to himself. The brocade curtain huddles round the glowing brazier; the six-petalled flowers of snowflakes offer their benison. There are few flowers that do not wither, but fresh scenes can be enjoyed all year round.

—Ji Cheng, *The Craft of Gardens*

◀ Snow transforms the grounds of the Summer Palace in winter.

# Dates of the Chinese Dynasties

| | |
|---|---|
| Xia Dynasty | 2070 – 1600 BC |
| Shang Dynasty | 1600 – 1046 BC |
| Zhou Dynasty | 1046 – 256 BC |
| Western Zhou Dynasty | 1046 – 771 BC |
| Eastern Zhou Dynasty | 770 – 256 BC |
| Spring and Autumn Period | 770 – 476 BC |
| Warring States Period | 475 – 221 BC |
| Qin Dynasty | 221 – 206 BC |
| Han Dynasty | 206 BC – 220 AD |
| Western Han Dynasty | 206 BC – 25 AD |
| Eastern Han Dynasty | 25 – 220 |
| Three Kingdoms | 220 – 280 |
| Wei | 220 – 265 |
| Shu Han | 221 – 263 |
| Wu | 222 – 280 |
| Jin Dynasty | 265 – 420 |
| Western Jin Dynasty | 265 – 316 |
| Eastern Jin Dynasty | 317 – 420 |
| Northern and Southern Dynasties | 420 – 589 |
| Southern Dynasties | 420 – 589 |
| Northern Dynasties | 439 – 581 |
| Sui Dynasty | 581 – 618 |
| Tang Dynasty | 618 – 907 |
| Five Dynasties and Ten States | 907 – 960 |
| Five Dynasties | 907 – 960 |
| Ten States | 902 – 979 |
| Song Dynasty | 960 – 1279 |
| Northern Song Dynasty | 960 – 1127 |
| Southern Song Dynasty | 1127 – 1279 |
| Liao Dynasty | 916 – 1125 |
| Jin Dynasty | 1115 – 1234 |
| Xixia Dynasty (or Tangut) | 1038 – 1227 |
| Yuan Dynasty | 1279 – 1368 |
| Ming Dynasty | 1368 – 1644 |
| Qing Dynasty | 1644 – 1911 |